Extreme Cuisine
Baby Bug Dishes

by Meish Goldish

Consultants:
David George Gordon, author of *The Eat-a-Bug Cookbook*
Andrew Zimmern, co-creator and host of *Bizarre Foods with Andrew Zimmern*

BEARPORT
PUBLISHING

New York, New York

Publisher: Kenn Goin
Editorial Director: Adam Siegel
Creative Director: Spencer Brinker
Design: Debrah Kaiser
Photo Researcher: Laura Saravia

Library of Congress Cataloging-in-Publication Data

Goldish, Meish.
   Baby bug dishes / by Meish Goldish.
      p. cm. — (Extreme cuisine)
   Includes bibliographical references and index.
   ISBN-13: 978-1-59716-758-1 (lib. binding)
   ISBN-10: 1-59716-758-4 (lib. binding)
   1. Cookery (Insects)—Juvenile literature. 2. Edible insects—Juvenile literature.
   3. Cookery, International—Juvenile literature. I. Title.

   TX746.G64 2009
   641.3—dc22

                              2008037435

For more information, write to Bearport Publishing Company, Inc., 101 Fifth Avenue, Suite 6R, New York, New York 10003. Printed in the United States of America.

10 9 8 7 6 5 4 3 2 1

MENU

Mealworm Spaghetti

The noodles on a plate of spaghetti can look a bit like wiggly worms. One Mexican cookbook, however, includes a dish in which it's not just the noodles that look like worms. It's the mealworms that are added as well!

To make mealworm spaghetti, a cook mixes boiled noodles with butter, salt, pepper, cheese, and almonds. Then the cook places roasted mealworms on top and serves the tasty dish.

Mealworms look like worms. Yet they are actually the **larvae**, or young form, of darkling beetles. People around the world dine on mealworms and other young insects. Although baby bugs aren't for everyone, in many countries they help turn an ordinary dish into a delicious one!

darkling beetle

mealworms

It takes four to five months for a mealworm to turn into an adult darkling beetle.

Fried Bamboo Worms

Many people begin their meals with a salad or a bowl of soup. In Thailand, some people start with a plate of fried bamboo worms. These little creatures aren't actually worms, however. They are moth larvae that live inside bamboo. To cook them, people in Thailand fry the young bugs. The salty and crispy treats are the perfect way to begin a meal.

bamboo worms

Insect larvae aren't just tasty, they're often healthful, too. Many larvae have lots of protein, which the human body uses to build bone and muscle.

Barbecued Grubs

When it's time for a cookout, people often grill ribs, chicken, hot dogs, or hamburgers. Some people in Indonesia, however, like to barbecue a different kind of meat. They grill baby Capricorn beetles called sago **grubs**.

To get the grubs, villagers in eastern Indonesia chop down a palm tree and grab the fat grubs from inside the trunk. They then slide the juicy insects onto sharp sticks and barbecue them. The baby beetles taste like fatty bacon with very chewy skin.

Some villagers in eastern Indonesia use grubs to clean their ears. They hold the baby bugs by their tails as the grubs slip inside the ears and eat the wax.

barbecued
sago grubs

Cheese Maggots

Who likes flies in their cheese? Some people on the Italian island of Sardinia do. They make cheese by leaving it out in the sun so that flies can lay their eggs in it. When the eggs hatch, thousands of **maggots** live in the cheese. As the young flies feed on the cheese it becomes creamy and smelly. In fact, the name of this food, *casu marzu*, means "rotten cheese."

People need to be careful when eating *casu marzu*. The wiggling maggots can jump up to six inches (15 cm), so some people wear eye protection when they eat the rotten cheese.

adult cheese fly

cheese fly maggot

When the maggots stop wiggling in *casu marzu*, it is a sign that the cheese has gone bad and is no longer safe to eat.

casu marzu

Mopane Worm Snacks

An old saying goes, "The early bird catches the worm." Yet in Botswana and South Africa, some people catch "worms," too—mopane (moh-PAH-nee) worms. These wiggly creatures are actually the larvae, or caterpillars, of emperor moths.

Villagers collect mopane worms by pulling them off the trees where they feed. They then squeeze out the insides of the caterpillars and put the dead insects in a bucket. The bugs are later boiled in salty water, dried out, and eaten as a snack. Sometimes the caterpillars are used in stews. Mopane worms are so popular that collecting and selling them is a big business in parts of southern Africa.

squeezing out the insides of mopane worms

South Africans eat so many mopane worms that scientists fear there may soon be no more of them left.

dried mopane worms

Baby Wasp Treats

Many people run away from wasps to keep from getting stung. In Japan, however, wasp hunters try to get as close to them as possible. They tie long silk threads to adult wasps so that they can follow the insects back to their nests. The hunters then use smoke to force the adult wasps out of their homes so that they can collect the tasty wasp larvae that are left inside.

Some restaurants in the Japanese city of Tokyo serve boiled wasp larvae. If you want to try some, just ask the waiter for *hachi-no-ko*.

adult wasp

14

People in Japan also like to eat deep-fried wasp larvae as a crunchy treat.

Stir-Fried Silkworms

Silkworms are little creatures that make silk. In parts of China, they also make a tasty meal.

Silkworms are the larvae, or young form, of silkworm moths. Like all larvae, these worm-like creatures hatch from eggs. About 27 days later, they begin spinning a silk shell around themselves. The insects are called **pupae** at this stage. They will grow wings, **antennae**, and legs inside their shells. Before that happens, however, workers in Suzhou, a city in eastern China, boil the pupae and strip off their silk shells. The young insects are now ready to become a meal. Some people in China love to stir-fry them in oil with onion, ginger, and garlic.

silk cocoon with pupa inside

The shell that a silkworm makes is called a cocoon.

Roasted Ant Eggs

Chicken eggs are eaten all over the world. Yet those are not the only kind of eggs that people eat. In the eastern part of Colombia, South America, ant eggs are considered a treat.

To collect the eggs, villagers wait until it rains. Why? The water flows into the insects' underground nest. It forces the ants to leave their home so that they don't drown. People can then collect the large females that have eggs inside them. To cook the ants, villagers wrap them in leaves and place them on a log near a fire. Then they bite into the roasted ants along with the eggs inside them.

Many people say that ants have a nutty taste.

roasted ants

Waxworm Salad

Most Americans don't eat insects. Yet some people are willing to give them a try. Each year, a "BugFest" is held in Raleigh, North Carolina. Visitors there dine on waxworm salad, which is made with the larvae of wax moths. They also eat mealworms cooked in tomato sauce.

Americans across the country already enjoy baby peas and carrots. Maybe someday they'll eat baby bugs, too!

waxworm

waxworm salad

Adult insects are also eaten at the BugFest. One dish people can try is stir-fried grasshoppers served over rice.

Where Are They Eaten?

Here are some of the places where baby bug dishes are eaten.

Waxworm Salad
United States

Cheese Maggots
Sardinia, Italy

Stir-Fried Silkworms
China

Boiled Wasp Larvae
Japan

Arctic Ocean

North America

Europe

Asia

Atlantic Ocean

Africa

Pacific Ocean

Pacific Ocean

South America

Indian Ocean

N
W E
S

Australia

Southern Ocean

Antarctica

Mealworm Spaghetti
Mexico

Roasted Ant Eggs
Colombia

Mopane Worms
Botswana and South Africa

Fried Bamboo Worms
Thailand

Barbecued Grubs
Indonesia

Glossary

antennae (an-TEN-ee)
the two body parts on an insect's head used for feeling and smelling

grubs (GRUHBZ)
the worm-like form of young beetles

larvae (LAR-vee)
the worm-like form of many kinds of young insects

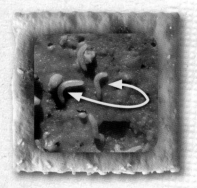

maggots (MAG-uhts)
the worm-like form of young flies

pupae (PYOO-pee)
young insects in a form between larvae and adults; they are usually enclosed in a cocoon

Index

Bibliography

Gordon, David George. *The Eat-a-Bug Cookbook: 33 Ways to Cook Grasshoppers, Ants, Water Bugs, Spiders, Centipedes, and Their Kin.* Berkeley, CA: Ten Speed Press (1998).

Menzel, Peter, and Faith D'Aluisio. *Man Eating Bugs: The Art and Science of Eating Insects.* Berkeley, CA: Ten Speed Press (1998).

Ramos-Elorduy, Julieta. *Creepy Crawly Cuisine: The Gourmet Guide to Edible Insects.* Rochester, VT: Park Street Press (1998).

Read More

Miller, Connie Colwell. *Disgusting Foods.* Mankato, MN: Capstone Press (2007).

Solheim, James. *It's Disgusting and We Ate It!: True Food Facts from Around the World and Throughout History.* New York: Simon & Schuster (2001).

Learn More Online

To learn more about baby bug dishes, visit **www.bearportpublishing.com/ExtremeCuisine**

About the Author

Meish Goldish has written more than 100 books for children. He lives in Brooklyn, New York.